Cheesy Wotsits and the History of Western Philosophy

Cheesy Wotsits and the History of Western Philosophy

Brian Luff

Fit2Fill Limited

Cheesy Wotsits & the History of Western Philosophy

This first edition published 2011 by Fit2Fill Limited,
7 Bourne Court, Southend Road, Woodford Green, IG8 8HD

© Copyright Brian Luff 2011

No parts of this publication may be produced, stored in or introduced into a retrieval system, or transmitted in any form or by any means such as electronic, mechanical, or otherwise without the prior permission of the
author and publisher.

All rights in this piece are strictly reserved and application for public reading or staging must be made by email to mail@pepperstock.co.uk. No performance may be given unless a licence has been obtained.

Cover photograph: Fotolia
Graphics/Illustrations: Brian Luff / Dreamstime

ISBN 978-1-4478-5127-1

"Nothing is something too."

Contents

Introduction	9
Toast Is Not Enough	15
Cheesy Wotsits	28
The Meaning of Pog	51
The Rule of Three	73
Cat Not Here	83
The Writer	105

Introduction

Zen teaches us that no snowflake ever falls in the wrong place. Try telling that to Transport for London.

It has been said that a man with one watch knows what time it is, whereas a man with two watches is never quite sure. A man with thirty watches or more has obviously just returned from a holiday in Bangkok.

And that, ladies and gentlemen, is philosophy.

Philosophy is like going to the dentist. We put off thinking about it for as long as we can but we know that sooner or later we're going to have to pay it a visit. And when we finally get around to it the process is usually made more bearable by the use of drugs.

So, why *are* we here? What *is* the meaning of existence? For me personally, there are three big philosophical questions that are as troubling as the dentist's drill.

One: "Why does there have to be anything at all? Why can't there just be nothing?"

Two: "Why did I ever have a relationship with a woman called Sue Whitstable?"

And the third, and by far most the important question of all, is this: "Why do we need Cheesy Wotsits?"

Now, these three things may not appear, at first sight, to be connected at all. But they are. And that's because, as we all know, *everything* is connected. The tricky bit is finding the connections.

To do that we have to cut through the clutter. Because the cosmos, quite simply, has got too much stuff in it.

It's a bit like my flat. The universe has got loads and loads of content that we don't really need. We probably don't need Black Holes for example. Basically, they're in the way.

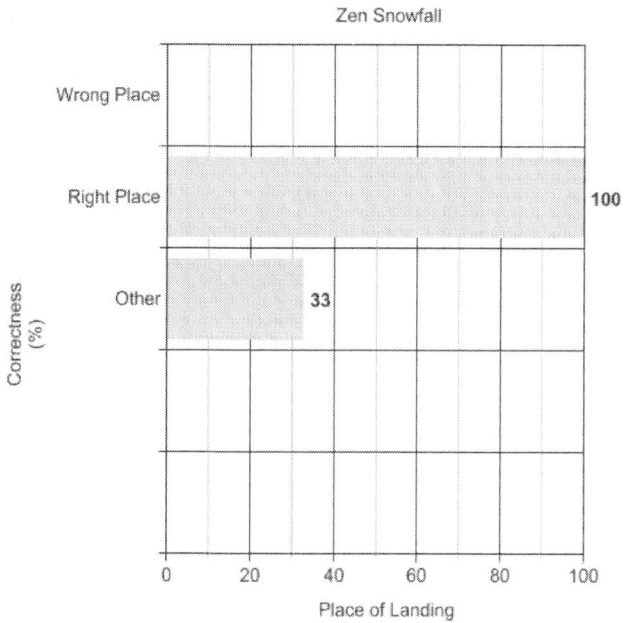

The entire universe doesn't actually *need* to be here at all. However, mathematicians tell us that it's physically impossible for the universe to *not* exist, because in mathematics you can't *not* get *something*. Even if it's zero. Even if the answer is nothing at all.

But should we trust mathematics? A philosopher once said "If a man who cannot count finds a four-leaf clover, is he still lucky?" My guess is that however shit we are at maths, that doesn't stop it from affecting our lives.

And while you're thinking about that, why don't you pick up the phone and make an appointment to see the dentist.

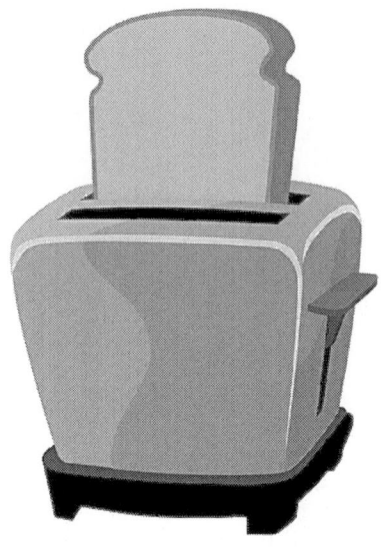

There are infinitely more possible ways for toast to exist than no toast.

1) Toast Is Not Enough

Lewis Carroll, who wrote Alice in Wonderland, was an expert on storytelling, and he left us an invaluable piece of advice.

He said "Begin at the beginning, go on until you come to the end, then stop." So that's what I'm going to do. I will start at the beginning.

At the beginning I knew very little about philosophy. Then I met a woman called Sue Whitstable. I was recently divorced at the time and rather unwisely thought I'd try a little bit of internet dating.

Internet dating is like Russian Roulette, except that there's a bullet in all the chambers and every single one of them usually results in a bang.

There was no speed dating then. You had to date people very, very slowly. I went out with a number of women. The ones I liked didn't like me, and the ones who liked me looked like Danny De Vito.

Then I met Sue Whitstable. I liked her. She liked me. She didn't look like Danny De Vito.

Sue was a student of philosophy. A mature student. We met on a web site for clever people. I lied about my I.Q. and Sue Whitstable lied about her age.

We went for long walks together on Hampstead Heath, and during those warm summer strolls, Sue Whitstable taught me all about Western philosophy - even though I didn't really want to know about Western philosophy.

When I met Sue she was wearing a T-shirt which read "Wittgenstein: True or False?" I said I thought that was very witty, so Sue thought I was clever. The next time I saw her she bought me a T-shirt which said exactly the same thing.

There is nothing worse than a couple who wear matching clothes, so I pretended to lose it. I said the washing machine had eaten it.

It was many months before I plucked up the courage to ask Sue what the T-shirt actually meant. She asked why I had called it "witty" if I didn't know what it meant, and I made up some lie about seeing a documentary about Wittgenstein on BBC4.

In case you're wondering, Wittgenstein was an Austrian philosopher who held the professorship in philosophy at Cambridge in the thirties and forties.

He landed the post because they were looking for someone with a German accent. In the nineteen thirties all scientists and philosophers had to have German accents. It was compulsory. Had Einstein come from Bristol his theories are extremely unlikely to have been taken so seriously.

Wittgenstein invented something called Logical Positivism which is the most difficult discipline of philosophy to say when you're pissed.

Logical Positivism looked at things and labeled them either true, false or meaningless.

There's never been a TV game show called True, False or Meaningless but there should be. It could fill thousands of hours of daytime television and be presented by Hugh Dennis.

The opening sequence could go like this: Hugh Dennis is smug: True. Hugh Dennis is funny. False. Hugh Dennis is a fish: Meaningless!

Wittgenstein never devised a game show. If he had I'd have known what that T-shirt meant right from the word go. Because I am what is known as "a Philistine".

Basically, I only know about things if they're on TV. If philosophers appeared regularly in X-Factor or Big Brother I would by now have an honorary degree. Had Wittgenstein ever taken part in Strictly Come Dancing, I would be lecturing about it at Cambridge.

But I am a Philistine. I'd rather see "We Will Rock You" than the latest Sondheim at the Colosseum.

I prefer a prawn cocktail to lightly boiled quails eggs on asparagus, and I only go and see the Royal Philharmonic Orchestra if they are playing the music from *Star Wars*.

It took Sue Whitstable quite a while to realise that I was a Philistine. I think it was when she made Beef Wellington and I asked her to pass the Reggae Reggae Sauce.

Philosophy is not really for Philistines. But somehow I have accidentally gate-crashed the party, wearing hobnail boots and a T-shirt that says "Hugh Dennis is a Fish."

So, having lured me into being at least slightly interested in philosophy, Sue shared with me a very interesting theory. A theory that has messed with my mind ever since. It is the theory that "something" will always be more stable than "nothing".

This is apparently because in mathematical terms there's only one way for there to be nothing, whereas there are an infinite number of ways for there to be something.

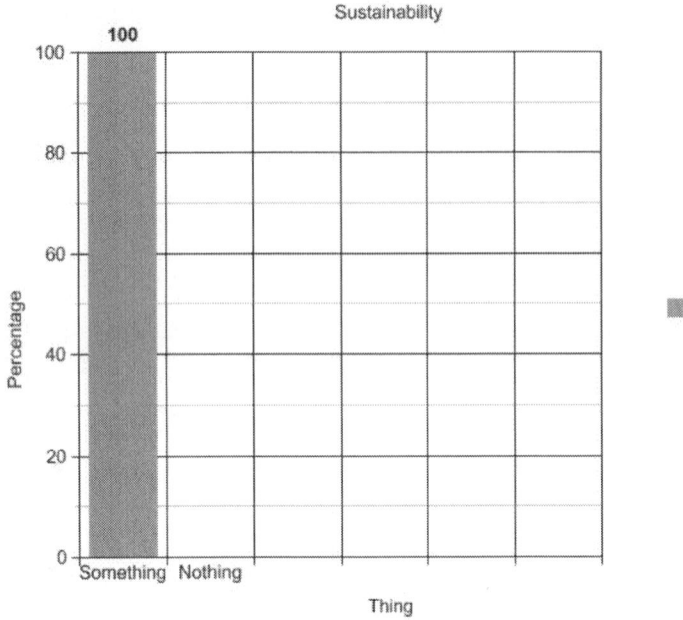

Now, I know that's a pretty big thing for you to get your head around, so if I may, I'm going to dumb that down for you. That doesn't imply that I think you are dumb, it just makes this whole thing a bit more accessible and I might sell more books.

Sue Whitstable always dumbed things down for me. But I think she did it because she genuinely thought I was a complete idiot.

So, there's only one way for there to be nothing, but an infinite number of ways for there to be something.

Take toast, for example. There's only one way for there to be *no* toast. Meanwhile, there are hundreds of ways for there to *be* toast. French toast, Melba toast, cheese on toast, burnt toast, toast that is only toasted on one side, toast that is toasted on both sides. I could go on, but then I would just want to go and eat some toast.

There are infinitely more possible ways for "toast" to exist than "no toast". And if there was no toast, we wouldn't be here talking about it in the first place. I'll be coming back to this theory at the end. I have a big finish.

It's also true to say that, "something" is more sustainable than "nothing", because "nothing" is inherently unstable. This is because there's isn't anything to move it forward or hold it together.

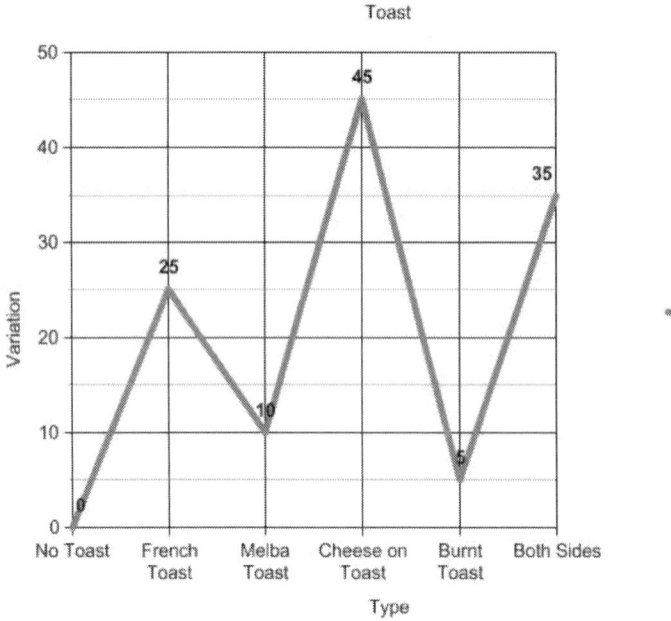

Which also means that nothing is something too. Because as soon as we *think* about nothing, it becomes something.

OK, now that I've planted that initial set of ideas in your head I'm going to expand upon them. I think the best way to do this is to give you a brief history of Western philosophy. I will obviously be dumbing that down as well, but hopefully you'll mistake this for irony and think the whole thing is very post-modern.

(We'll be hearing more about post-modernism later, and obviously we'll be dumbing that down as well.)

A Spanish philosopher called Antonio once said "A thing, until it is everything, is noise, and once it is everything it is silence."

To be honest I think that may have lost something in the translation, so we'll quickly draw a veil over that and move on.

As Sue Whitstable and I wandered over Parliament Hill Fields, and I tried to guess how old she really was, I myself reasoned that if "nothing" is really that unstable, then a *cluttered* cosmos must be more stable than an uncluttered cosmos.

But what is clutter? The dictionary definition is "a confusing or disorderly state or collection, and a possible symptom of compulsive hoarding."
I looked up compulsive hoarding and before long stumbled upon an organisation called Clutterers Anonymous.

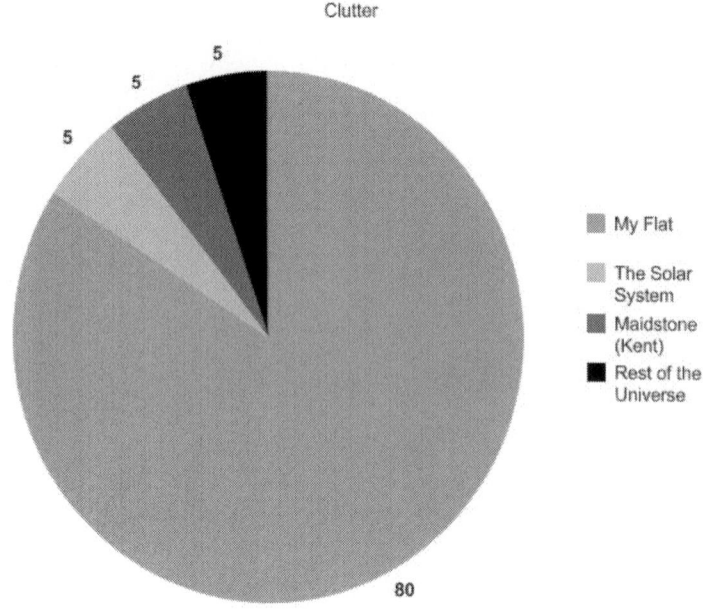

Apparently Clutterers Anonymous is a 12 step programme for people who have a problem with the accumulation of clutter. It has active meetings in 70 cities, and believes that cluttering behavior can be symptomatic of deeper issues. Problem clutterers are more likely to have depression, mania, OCD or ADHD.

ADHD is like AD but with much higher screen resolution.

Many experts attribute cluttering to the human desire to hunt and gather, while others describe it as a consequence of over-consumption.

Hunter-gathering was what they did in Tottenham High Road in August 2011. This led to chronic over-consumption of electronic goods and sports footware, and subsequent cluttering of the prison system.

Some members of Clutterers Anonymous describe the need to needlessly hunt and gather and the inability to subsequently let go of objects as a consequence of some kind of "spiritual emptiness". They're filling a void.

I once knew a man called Denis Gifford. He collected comics. He had comics in cupboards, comics under the sofa, and comics on the floor. He once told me that he even kept comics in the fridge.

Denis had kept every single comic he had bought since he was a small child. When I asked him why he did it he said, "Because no-one ever told me that you were supposed to throw them away."

Cluttering is a Health & Safety nightmare of course, and does tend to increase the frequency of trip hazards in the home. And Sod's Law of course states that if you can trip over something, you will trip over something. So clutter can potentially be fatal.

However, anything that's at odds with Health & Safety regulations can only be a good thing. Which is another large feather in the cap of clutter.

Despite all this negativity surrounding clutter, mathematics assures us that clutter is beneficial. A cluttered cosmos is more stable than an uncluttered cosmos. So clutter is good. Q.E.D.

2) Cheesy Wotsits

So where does Aesthetics fit into this tidy picture of an untidy universe? Let's begin by asking ourselves a simple question: Is clutter more beautiful than an absence of clutter? Can "nothing" ever be aesthetically pleasing?

For me, the words "Arsenal Nil" are beautiful, and they are clearly a mathematical expression of nothing.

Take *nouvelle cuisine*. This is essentially no food on a plate. More to the point, this is no food on a plate that costs more than *some* food on a plate. In other words the chef places as much value on the white space on the plate as he does on the food he cooks. So he clearly considers the *absence* of food to be aesthetically beautiful.

Minimalist design also appears to follow this principle. A designer shows up at your house. He removes all the furniture, paints the walls white, and hands you a bill for a hundred thousand pounds. He is therefore placing an aesthetic value on the absence of two things: The absence of your furniture, and the absence of money in your bank account.

A man called Charles Finn once said "Please listen carefully and try to hear what I am *not* saying. I tell you everything that is really nothing, and nothing of what is everything."

I have no idea what that means but shortly after saying that Charles Finn was elected to be the Conservative member of parliament for Henley-On-Thames. Not really.

So do all of these examples of nothingness destabilise the universe by removing the very clutter that holds reality together? It's possible, isn't it? A philosopher once said don't miss the donut by looking through the hole. I don't think that's relevant to this but its a nice image all the same.

What is really, really hard to swallow, is that according to this theory, the universe might be better off with "Arsenal one" than it is with "Arsenal nil".

And if we were to remove even one tiny thing from the cosmos - say, Cheesy Wotsits - then the universe would actually become more unstable. A less safe place in which to to live.

Can this be true? Do Cheesy Wotsits really help to hold the cosmos together? I emailed Nigel Parrott, former head of Golden Wonder, who invented Cheesy Wotsits, and I asked him that very question. But he didn't reply. Maybe he was at the dentist.

OK, so now that we have established the huge importance of Cheesy Wotsits to the cosmos, I suppose we'd better find out a bit more about them.

Firstly, and most importantly, I like Cheesy Wotsits. More specifically, I like *eating* Cheesy Wotsits. Sue Whitstable hated Cheesy Wotsits. They made her gag. Lots of things made her gag. But Cheesy Wotsits also brought Sue out in a rash. To Sue, a Cheesy Wotsit was the snack food equivalent of slowly scratching her fingernails down a blackboard. Or watching Richard & Judy on TV.

Cheesy Wotsits are a type of what scientists call "cheese puffs". The most common form are cheese flavoured curly shapes. However over the years various other shapes have been marketed.

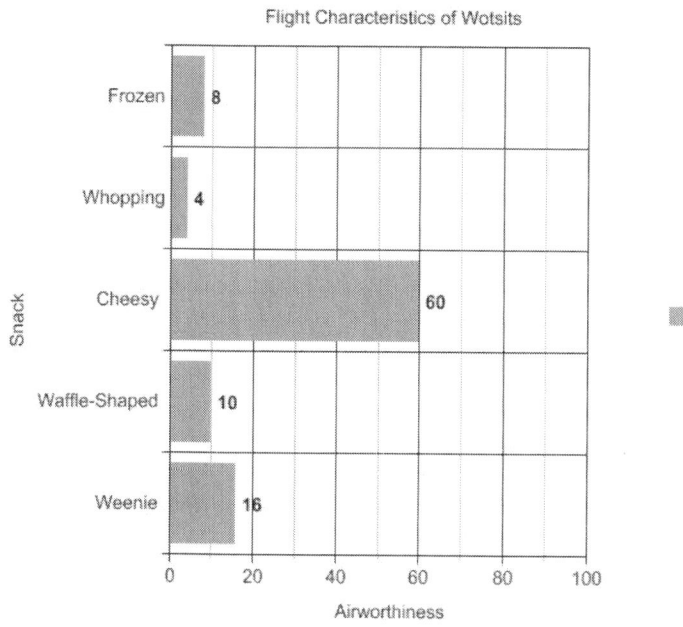

There have been waffle-shaped Wotsits, for example, but these didn't catch on because they not as aerodynamic as the originals. The air worthiness of a cheese puff may not be important to you, but it is extremely important if you happen to be a twelve year old boy in a school classroom.

I've always believed that all cheese snacks should be tested in wind tunnels in order to mazimise their use as projectiles during maths lessons.

There have been various flavours of Cheesy Wotsits such as prawn cocktail flavour and Flamin' Hot flavour. Limited edition Cheesy Wotsits have also appeared on more than one occasion. But Wikipedia says it needs a citation for this.

The Cheesy Wotsits brand has since been stretched into Whopping Wotsits, Weenie Wotsits, and Frozen Wotsits. Although why anyone would want to freeze a Wotsit I cannot possibly imagine.

One of a thing is no longer enough. For example there probably used to be only one type of yoghurt. Now are are about twenty thousand different types of yoghurt.

This simple little dairy product is breeding, and it's spreading and multiplying like a clowder of feral cats.

A clowder is the collective noun for cats. I probably didn't need to tell you that. But you have to remember, this is a dumbed down text.

Soon there will be a different type of yoghurt for every single human being on the planet. Why? Because all of this additional clutter naturally serves to make the universe more stable. So yoghurt, just like everything else in the universe, defaults to multiple forms. It can't help itself.

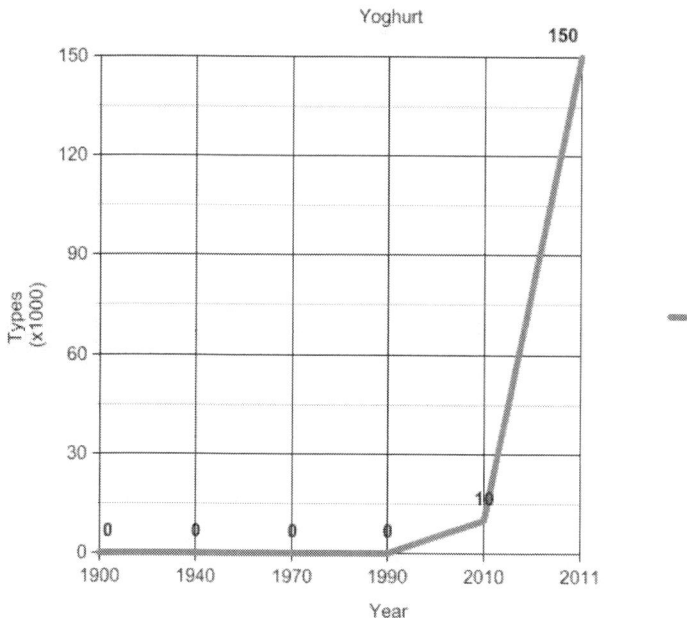

In exactly the same way, toilet cleaner defaults to multiple forms, even though there is very little difference between Tesco Active Gel and Harpic Power Plus. These products cannot help but multiply. The universe is calling to them. They are helpless to resist.

"Clutter me!" says the universe, "Clutter me!"

Even individual species of toilet cleaner will eventually evolve into multiple brands, so that in a thousand years time we could theoretically have an almost infinite number of types of Toilet Duck 3 in 1 Liquid Fresh.

"Why do we need so many different types of toilet cleaner?" the philosopher Socrates might have asked - acting as always as though he knew nothing at all about toilet cleaner, whereas he did really because he was so clever. His students would have tried to work out the reason, then they would have become confused and gone and made toast.

Sue Whitstable used over twenty different types of toilet cleaner. She also made her own yoghurt, which was disgusting. It tasted like garden compost and bogies.

From Sue Whitstable I learned a lot about toilet cleaner, yoghurt and Socrates, who was apparently convinced of the importance of having laws. There had to be laws about everything.

And since there were no laws about how many types of toilet cleaner or yoghurt you could have, Socrates would not have lost any sleep worrying about that.

Socrates was a *very* clever man. I mean, we are talking staggeringly clever. More clever than Steven Hawking. More clever than Professor Brian Cox. More clever, even, than Charlie Brooker.

Too smart for his own good as it turned out, because he was eventually arrested for being too clever. There wasn't actually a law about how clever you could be, but the State must have found a very neat legal loophole because Socrates was sentenced to death, and was put in prison.

Obviously he could have escaped if he'd wanted to, because he was probably the cleverest person to ever live.

But Socrates refused to escape because it was against the law. Instead he drank poison and died, rather than break the law.

How do we know all this? Because of the History Channel? No. Because of The One Show? No. It was because of Plato.

Sue Whitstable talked a lot about Plato as well. Usually while I was trying to watch Sky Sport. Plato probably knew very little about toilet cleaner or yoghurt but he did know an awful lot about Socrates, because he'd been a pupil of his.

Plato had wanted to drop philosophy and take geography and history instead, but his parents told him that philosophy would be a good thing to fall back on. He could always become a supply teacher and teach philosophy.

Plato protested furiously but then it was explained to him that he couldn't always have what he wanted. Because life wasn't perfect

Socrates was a very clever man.

As a result of this, Plato became obsessed with perfection. He came up with perfect examples of everything. The perfect house, the perfect flower, the perfect piece of toast. He said that they all existed but they were somehow out of reach. He said all we could see was their "shadowy reflections". He called them Platonic Forms.

I once told Sue Whitstable that I thought a Platonic Form was something you had to fill in if you were going to live with someone but not have sex with them. But Sue didn't get it.

Plato probably spent years trying to make the perfect piece of toast. But every time he thought he'd got it exactly right, he would turn his back for a moment and his partner would come into the kitchen and switch the toaster to a different setting. Which is what Sue Whitstable always did to me.

Eventually Plato got sick of trying to make the perfect piece of toast and instead wrote a book. He didn't have a publisher, but he wrote a book anyway.

The book was called The Republic and it starred his old teacher and drinking buddy Socrates, who in it, along with various other philosophy pundits, discussed the meaning of justice.

Plato asked if a good man was happier than a bad man. Sue Whitstable and I discussed this at length one evening on the Piccadilly Line. Sue reckoned the good man would be happier. I reckoned that it would depend on who the good man was and who the bad man was.

For example, I'm quite a good man , but despite of this fact I seem to spend most of the time depressed. Adolf Hitler, on the other hand, was a bad man, and he always appeared to be reasonably upbeat.

Plato might as well have compared a bald man to a man with loads of hair. Harry Hill: Bald. Happy and content. Fred West: Loads of hair. Serial Killer. It's just random.

Plato had strong views on what "nothing" was. He said that the definition of nothing was "That which rocks dream about."

I've thought about this quite a lot, and I don't think any of us can be absolutely sure what rocks dream about unless we use marijuana.

I used to use marijuana when I was younger, and I also used to have a pet rock. Pet rocks were very big in the eighties. Usually my pet rock sat quite still and was completely unemotional. But sometimes it was moved.

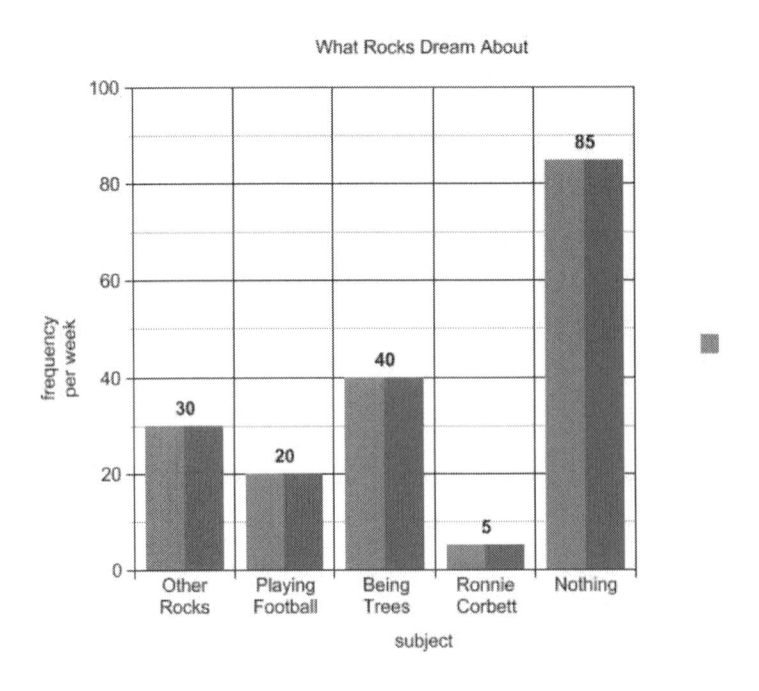

What Rocks Dream About

subject	frequency per week
Other Rocks	30
Playing Football	20
Being Trees	40
Ronnie Corbett	5
Nothing	85

How do we know that rocks do not have dreams? Maybe rocks dream about being trees. Maybe trees dream about being animals. Maybe animals dream about being human. Last night I dreamt about being Ronnie Corbett. Makes you think, doesn't it?

We need dreams. We're told that if we were to stop dreaming we would go mad. I don't know whether this is true but I am a constant sufferer of a disturbing occurrence known as *déjà vue*. This is when you feel like something has happened before, but you can't put your finger on where or how or when it happened.

Scientists believe that this is simply because your brain records something in two places at the same time, instead of in one place. So the first recording sees the second recording and thinks it's seeing a different occurrence.

But whatever the reason for it, *déjà vue* is a very disconcerting experience.

But back to nothingness. I typed "What is nothing?" into Yahoo Answers, and the most intelligent response that came back was "It's what's in-between your ears, you total dickhead!" Thanks for that... Sue.

Answers.com came up with a slightly better response. It said "Nothing is the name of an album by a Swedish thrash metal band called Meshuggah." I didn't even know they had thrash metal in Sweden, so that was actually quite interesting.

Not entirely unsurprisingly, the best definition I found for "nothing" was at Marijuana.com.

It was a post which said "Woh! Like, nothing is totally cool, man. PS. Everything is dying. PPS. Haven't we had this conversation before? PPPS. I'm hungry, have you got any Twiglets"

Plato also explored the role of poetry in society. Sue liked poetry and used to read it to me while I was in the bath trying to listen to Talk Sport.

I once suggested that Sue should go and write a poem about her yoghurt making. Unfortunately on one occasion she failed to see the irony and went and wrote one. Which I suppose served me right.

If you really want to fully understand the role of poetry in society I have just two words for you. Pam Ayres.

I don't really do poetry, but I do like science programmes. Science programmes were invented by a man called Aristotle a long time before there was anything to show them on.

Aristotle basically invented science. There would be no professor Professor Brian Cox if it were not for Aristotle. So Aristotle actually has rather a lot to answer for.

Last night I watched a science programme about dreams. We need dreams. We're told that if we were to stop dreaming we would go mad. I don't know whether this is true but I am a constant sufferer of a disturbing occurrence known as *déjà vue*.

This is when you feel like you've seen something before, but you can't quite put your finger on where or how or when it happened. Whatever the reason for it, *déjà vue* is a very disconcerting experience.

Aristotle said that if we want to learn about the world, we should do tests and look at the results. Like putting a Cheesy Wotsit in a wind tunnel.

For example, if we want to know what will happen if we put a kitten in a microwave, the best way to find out is to put a kitten in a microwave and write down the results. We can then compare our results to the results of other people who have put kittens in microwaves.

By the way, if you are going to perform that particular experiment yourself, don't forget to set up some control experiments. Without them the results will be meaningless. My suggestions for control experiments are a kitten in a microwave without the microwave switched on, an empty microwave, and a kitten sitting on a nice comfortable cushion, three miles away from the nearest microwave.

Sue Whitstable had a kitten. But unfortunately she didn't have a microwave.

Plato may have invented science but he was shit at it. Particularly astronomy. He was really, really shit at astronomy. For a start, he thought that the Earth was flat and was in the middle of universe. He also surmised that Hell was underneath us, and that all the stars and the planets and the Sun were going around us. It might have been wrong but this view of the universe actually lasted for the next sixteen hundred years.

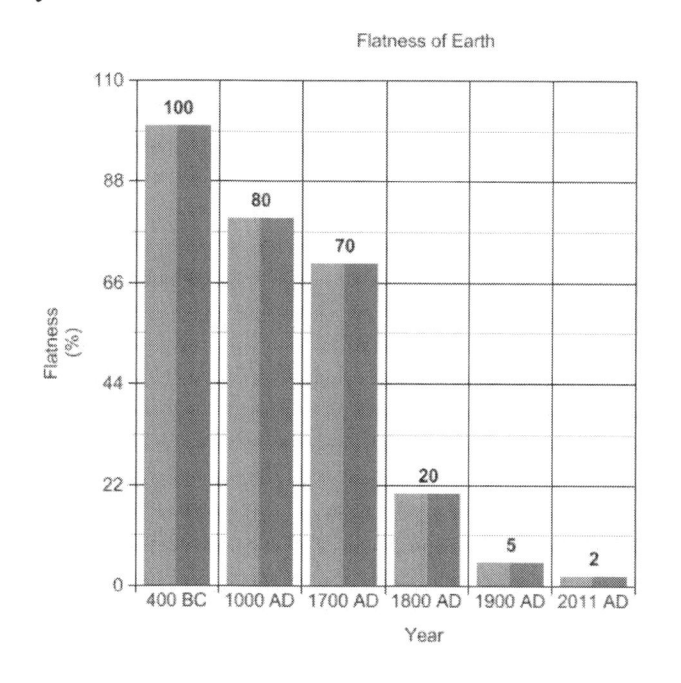

Flatness of Earth

Year	Flatness (%)
400 BC	100
1000 AD	80
1700 AD	70
1800 AD	20
1900 AD	5
2011 AD	2

Amazingly, the Flat Earth Society is still around today. It even has a web site. Last time I checked the website was down, which I think should tell you quite a lot about the commitment of its members.

The Flat Earth Society was founded by a guy called Samuel Rowbotham in the early 1800's. He was an English inventor. I'm not sure what he invented, but I'm guessing that it was stupidity.

Sam's views were based largely on literal interpretation of the Bible. Which is never a good place to start. You need to unzip your mind before you can start putting forward theories.

Sam used his considerable scientific and astronomical skills to state that the earth was a flat disk centered at the North Pole and bounded along its southern edge by a great wall of ice, with the sun, moon, planets, and stars only a few hundred miles above the surface of the earth.

After Sam's death, Flat Earth theory quickly spread to the United States of America where it became immensely popular. There's a surprise.

Unsurprisingly a large part of middle-America still believes the theory to this day.

They've also never heard of Professor Brian Cox and they think Charles Darwin was a blasphemer who should have been burnt at the stake. And they listen to country music and Iron Maiden.

The International Flat Earth Society was founded in 1956 by another Sam, Samuel Shenton, who bizarrely was a member of the Royal Astronomical Society as well. A very learned man, my theory is that he thought that there simply weren't enough societies in the world. Not enough clutter. So he started another one.

I've started the Cheesy Wotsits Society. We believe that the earth and all the planets revolve around a huge curly shaped cheese puff at the centre of the universe.

Who's to say that isn't true? Because there are infinitely more ways for something to exist than nothing.

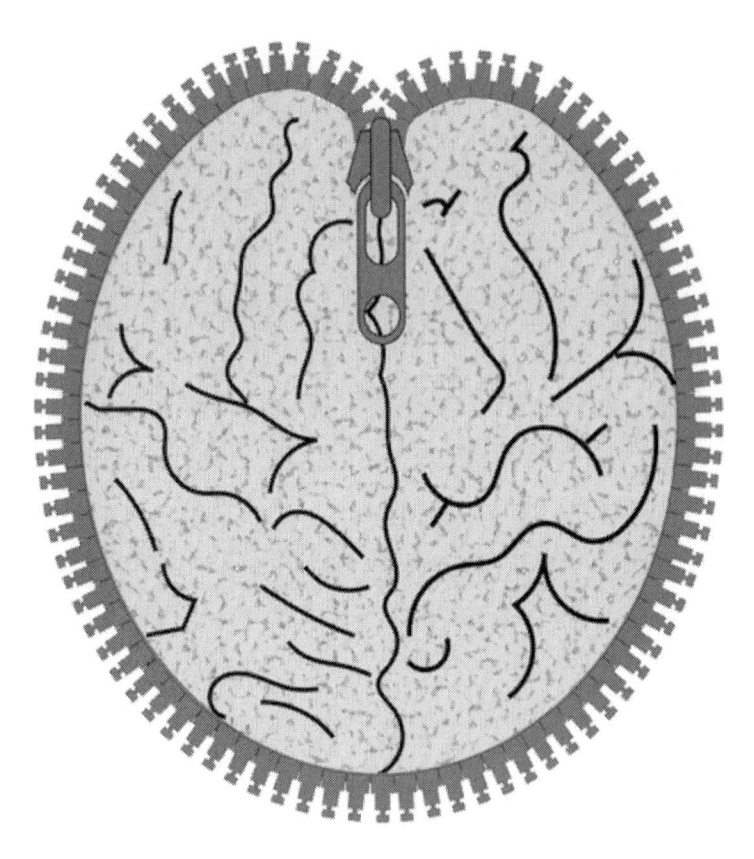

You need to unzip your mind before you can start putting forward theories.

Mathematically there are multiple ways in which a Cheesy Wotsit could be the centre of the Solar System, whereas there's only one way for the Cheesy Wotsit to not be there.

And the implications of that are far, far greater than you think. Stick around for that big finish.

3) The Meaning of Pog

After we'd been going out for a couple of months, Sue Whitstable moved her toothbrush into my flat. A few days later she moved everything else. Two van loads.

My nice uncluttered little flat became filled with stuff I didn't need. More to the point, Sue Whitstable didn't need the vast majority of it either.

Most of the contents of Sue's one bedroom flat in Kilburn now seemed to be under my bed. Some of it was so old that the plastic bags in which it was stored were starting to biodegrade.

There were books, audio cassettes, video cassettes, and numerous forms of stored content for which the playback device was no longer manufactured.

There were hundreds of floppy discs. You can't even put a floppy disc into a computer anymore. Even if you could, nowadays a floppy disc would be too small to store the contents of an email. But Sue Whitstable wanted the floppy discs, so the floppy discs stayed under my bed, along with about seven hundred paperbacks on the subject of philosophy.

Then, nothing much happened for a while. In fact, nothing much happened for a very, very, long time. Sue Whitstable and I got into a rut. We watched TV. We went for walks. We went to the dentist. We made various types of toast. Sue made yoghurt. I ate Cheesy Wotsits, and Sue continued to educate me about toilet cleaner and philosophy, even though I was much more interested in football.

Our next point of call was the Renaissance, which was first alluded to during a Champions League quarter final, second leg.

During the Renaissance, it seemed that a chap called Machiavelli wrote a book called The Prince, in which he described how a ruler should rule. It said things like "If you slap a man in the face, then he's liable to slap you back. However, if you cut off both his arms, then he can't slap you."

I told Sue Whitstable that this was a daft idea and she slapped me in the face. When I jokingly suggested that I ought to cut off both her arms she slapped me in the face again. But much, much harder. Which is a very good example of unsuccessful use of philosophy in the field.

Meanwhile, I was becoming increasingly interested in nothingness. When I told this to Sue, she said that a good place to learn about nothingness was in the writings of Jean-Paul Sartre? He apparently wrote a book called *Being and Nothingness.*

Before I met Sue I'd only heard Jean-Paul Sartre mentioned in sketches by Monty Python. Jean-Paul was an existentialist, which is the discipline of philosophy which is the second most difficult to say when you're pissed.

Sartre was only five foot two, and when you're that short the only way you're ever going to get laid is by being very, very clever. So Jean-Paul sat up and paid attention when he was at school.

Sartre's eyes looked in completely different directions, so you never really knew in which direction he was philosophising.

He published *Being and Nothingness* in 1943, and this book would appear to be the most miserable and bleak view of life that philosophy has ever thrown up.

Basically it states that Man is separate from the world, and that his existence is nothing more than pointless, futile absurdity. In other words, clutter. We ourselves are clutter, according to Jean-Paul Sartre.

Another of Sartre's cheerful little books was a novel called *Nausea*. This was the story of a man having a nervous breakdown. The high point of this book was when the man picked up a pebble on the beach and became painfully aware that it was a pebble. He found its pebbliness overwhelming. Then the poor chap became overwhelmed by the realness of his own hands. He sat and stared at his hands. He became hypnotised by his hands. For a while he mistook his hands for crabs, then he realised that they were not crabs, they were hands. Then he thought they were crabs again. This went on for quite a while. Hands. Crabs. Crabs. Hands.

Existentialism believes that like crabs we have an outer shell. But our shells are not filled with delicious crab meat. They are filled with consciousness that allows us to think about what we are doing while we are doing it. Like when we are looking at our hands and mistaking them for crabs.

Jean-Paul also believed that we were free to make choices - even if this meant doing nothing. In fact he was at great pains to point out that doing nothing is a perfectly valid life choice in itself.

Ah, but what *is* doing nothing? Can we ever truly be sure that we are doing nothing? Maths says no. Because we've now established that even nothing is something. So, even if you're doing nothing, you're actually doing something. Ask any professional actor, and he will tell you that this is true.

Sartre taught us that no matter how much you might want to deny it, your life is what you make it. For good or for bad you have free will, and you have no-one else to blame but yourself. Unless you're an actor of course, in which case you can blame your agent.

In later life Sartre abandoned the idea of writing bleak, depressing literature and decided instead to simply lead a bleak and depressing life. If only he'd been a couple of inches taller, perhaps he'd have been happier and would not have tried quite so hard.

But onto more important things. Pogs. Did I mention that I once collected pogs? Some of you may know what a "pog" is, but for the rest I will explain. There will be no need to dumb this bit down because pogs are pretty dumb in the first place.

Cheesy Wotsits was one of the first crisp brands to introduce small toys into its packs, and they did this by the clever insertion of pogs.

Pogs look a bit like flat plastic bottle caps, and they can be printed with a picture of anything from Superman to Britney Spears. I had a set of pogs with the faces of all the characters from the Simpsons, for example. Pogs is also the name of a game that you can play using these objects.

The name originates from a brand of fruit juice called POG which was made from passion fruit, orange and guava, and the use of the POG bottle caps to play the game actually pre-dates the game's commercialization. Which is very interesting. But only if you collect pogs.

The game of Pogs probably originated in Hawaii in the 1930s or possibly has its origins in a game from much earlier called Menko, which is a Japanese game very similar to Pogs. So, pogs have been in existence for at least 300 years, and may even be much, much older.

Who knows, Socrates may have played Pogs with Plato. "How should Pogs be played?" Socrates may have asked his student.
"I think you probably know the answer to that already," Plato would have replied.

Pog.

The game of Pogs hit a huge peak of popularity in the 1990's when the World POG Federation was formed and they introduced Pogs to the world via bags of Cheesy Wotsits. In the game of Pogs each player has their own collection of pogs and a slammer, which is a heavier piece made of metal.

Before the game, the players decide whether they're going to to play "for keeps", or not for keeps.

"For keeps" implies that the players keep the pogs that they win and forfeit those that have been won by other players.

The game then begins as follows: You make a stack of pogs to play with by putting them on top of each other. Each player must pile the same number of pogs to their own stack to make it fair. You can stack them face up or face down. Face down is the most advisable.

Decide which player is going first then that player "whacks the stack". This means that he throws the slammer at the stack. This sends pogs flying everywhere.

All the pogs that land face up go to the player who whacked the stack. The rest are re-stacked and the next player has a go with the slammer. This continues until all the pogs have been flipped over and won.

The player with the most pogs at the end of the game is the winner.

The pog craze soared in the 1990's, and then it rapidly faded out. And now you know why. Because Pogs is probably the most stupid game ever invented.

Pog Collecting

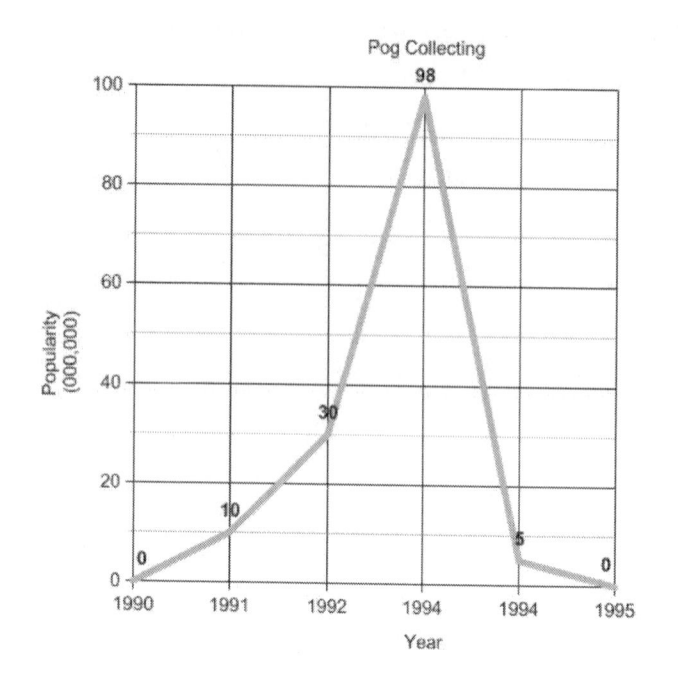

Year	Popularity (000,000)
1990	0
1991	10
1992	30
1994	98
1994	5
1995	0

Which means that all of the pogs in the world are needless clutter. A complete waste of plastic. Ah, but we now know that the more clutter we have in the cosmos, the more stable the universe becomes. So, because of pogs we're that little bit further away from oblivion.

OK, now we understand why pogs are such a vital cog in the great gearwheel of the universe.

When I played Pogs with Sue Whitstable she wanted to play for keeps. I wasn't entirely happy about that, but I played for keeps all the same.

It took Sue Whitstable only 10 minutes to win a collection of pogs it had taken me over ten years to assemble. Which wouldn't have been terrible in itself. But the following weekend, while I was at a football match, Sue Whitstable took all of the pogs she had won from me and she threw them into the dustbin.

In doing this, she fractionally reduced the amount of clutter in the cosmos and effectively made the universe more unstable. She also made me more unstable.

I'm not sure of many things but I am sure that I will never forgive Sue Whitstable for doing that.

The philosopher Descartes spent years wondering what he could be sure of, but surely even Descartes would have been 100% sure that Sue Whitstable should not have thrown my pogs into the dustbin.

"I think, therefore I am absolutely certain that Sue Whitstable should not have thrown my pogs into the bin." René Descartes

The whole outside world may be an illusion. The only thing you can absolutely know for sure is your own thoughts.

"I think, therefore I am absolutely certain that Sue Whitstable should not have thrown my pogs into the bin."

Descartes was of course a truly great mathematician and philosopher. He was the first person to ask the question "What is the relationship between the mind and the body?"

Once again, this depends entirely on who the mind and the body belong to. What, for example, is the relationship between the mind and the body of Katie Price? Great body. Shit mind. In Professor Stephen Hawking we of course have the exact opposite configuration.

I know the relationship between my own mind and my own body very well. It's flaky, to say the least. An extremely unstable and unreliable relationship.

Most of the time my mind is completely unable to control my body at all. Particularly when it comes to eating food, drinking alcohol, or taking healthy exercise.

On a daily basis my mind asks my body very politely to not do something. My body thinks about it for a nano-second, then promptly turns around to my mind and says "Fuck off!"

My mind asks again, and this time my body gives it a slap around the face. My mind then suggests that it should cut off my body's hands, and my body gives my mind an even bigger slap.

So now we're field testing both Descartes and Machiavelli at the same time. Be it only in a very dumbed down way. We have once again learned that philosophy is of very little use when you're being slapped around the face.

But what is the relationship between the mind and the body? Sadly, science will never be able to answer that question because science is way too objective. Our minds, however, are not. They are totally subjective, and known only to us.

As you get older your mind matures while at the same time your body decays. It's one of the great ironies of life. Your appreciation of sensual beauty increases while your ability to do anything about it decreases.

The most common view is that the solution to the whole mind & body conundrum will never be found by the mind because the mind *itself* is part of the conundrum. It's like the Metropolitan Police setting up a special unit to investigate corruption in the Metropolitan Police. You can't solve the problem if you're part of the problem.

"But what of Kant?" I hear you ask. Surely one of the most popular philosophers of the eighteenth century and he hasn't had a look in so far.

Well, Sue had a problem with Kant. She'd once spent six weeks writing a paper on Kant and on the day she was due to hand it in her computer crashed and she lost the lot.

So Immanuel Kant was *persona non grata* in our house. Unless I wanted to annoy Sue. Which was quite a lot. I would sometimes Google Kant and quote him, out of the blue, during meal times.

Kant was all about something called Absolutism: Actions evaluated by logically examining the motives behind them. This was also the philosophy of Mr Spock: An action is permissible if its motive is logically coherent. For example "Why should I be moral?" The answer is that to be immoral is irrational. Pure Mr Spock. But Kant believed that only humans beings were rational, and Mr Spock is not a human being.

Mentioning Kant was unexceptable at the best of times in our house. Aligning Kant with a character from *Star Trek* was tantamount to a declaration of war.

"Why must you dumb everything down?" Sue would scream. But she didn't understand. *Star Trek* is not dumbing down. *Star Trek*, if anything, is dumbing up. If you're a Philistine.

There are probably more Trekkies in the world than there are Buddhists. Kant had Universal Laws, *Star Trek* had the Prime Directive - the most prominent guiding principle of the United Federation of Planets.

The Prime Directive dictated that there can be no interference with the internal development of alien civilizations. Meanwhile, Kant had The Categorical Imperative which determined whether an action is morally permissible.

OK, best way to settle it? Kant v Mr Spock. Pogs. Best out of three. Play for keeps.

Maybe that's why Sue threw my Pogs away. I'd never really thought about that. Maybe she did it as revenge for me talking about Immanuel Kant during meal times.

On second thoughts... Spock would probably rather play Kant at three dimensional chess.

Sue also had issues with Gottfried Leibniz. This is because she didn't agree with what he said, and frankly neither do I. Leibniz was a German philosopher and mathematician. He wrote primarily in Latin but no-one in Germany could understand Latin so he had to have everything translated into German.

Leibniz seems to me to be the master of "Stating the Bleeding Obvious". For example he worked for about ten years to prove that if a fact is true, then the opposite of that fact is false. He then laboured for another ten years to prove that the theory also works the other way around.

He then moved on to things that are different from each other and things that are the same as each other. He began by saying that if two things are identical, if they are completely identical, then they are the same.

He then said that if two things are non-identical, and do not share any similarity whatsoever, then they are not the same.

This is referred to as Leibniz's Law and has attracted much controversy and criticism, particularly from people who believe that two identical things are not the same.

In his later years, Leibniz starting working with three things, but his mind became cluttered and he got confused. At this point he started watching Sesame Street,

Leibniz's *piece de resistance* was the theory that there must be sufficient reason for a thing to exist. This theory has also been challenged, and rightly so. I've been watching for ten years and I still can't find sufficient reason for the existence of Kerry Katona.

Of course not all philosophers were geniuses. Every profession has its bullshit merchants. In the professional of philosophy this position was admirably filled by a man called Heraclitus, who lived around 500 BC. He only wrote one book. It was called *On Nature*, and it was filled with the most cynical, time-serving, piss-taking waffle you've ever read in your life.

Cosmology, politics, theology - Heraclitus could bullshit about all of them. Not surprisingly, history remembers him as the "obscure" philosopher.

His philosophy was so ambiguous it could be applied to almost anything. He claimed that he did this on purpose so that people might apply his thoughts and theories to their own lives, whoever they were, wherever they lived, however half-witted they were.

When Socrates read his book he said, "The concepts that I understand are great. The concepts that I don't understand are great too."

Hey, if Socrates didn't understand it, it was either pure genius or complete bollocks. I'll let you form your own opinion.

He began with the fairly safe and innocuous concept that "everything flows". If we'd wanted to know that we could have simply asked a hippy.

He said that many people fail to notice what they do after they wake up, just as they forget what they do while they are asleep. He added "What we see when we are asleep... is sleep."

He qualified this by saying that for those who are awake, there is one common universe, and that thinking is common to all.

Heraclitus also had some very precise philosophy about the animal kingdom. Donkeys would choose rubbish rather than gold. Pigs enjoy mud. Fish drink sea water while humans cannot. Here's the best one: "Dogs bark at those they do not recognise."

"I have noticed that dogs bark at strangers. I am therefore a philosopher."

This man was basically writing the first thing that came into his head. I'm guessing that in those days philosophers got paid by the word.

"The way up, and the way down are one and the same thing," he said.

The overriding message seemed to be that everything is common to something else, and ideally everything is the reversal of something else.

"From all things one, and from one, all things. Immortals are mortal, mortals immortal. The sane are insane and the insane are sane. Dogs are small hairy animals and small hairy animals are dogs. My bellend is purple, and purple is my bellend."

So much for Heraclitus.

4) The Rule of Three

Now, I'm sure you will have heard of all or most of the philosophers I've mentioned so far. This is all fairly mainstream stuff. But there are also some delightfully obscure philosophies knocking around in the world.

One of the books that Sue stuffed under my bed was all about something called Arianism - the theory that there is no Christian Trinity. In other words, there's a Father, a Son but no Holy Ghost.

I don't know what Arianism had against the poor old Holy Ghost, but this theory actually has a far more sinister implication. It breaks the Rule of Three.

You cannot break the Rule of Three. The Rule of Three is sacred. Three Lions on the Shirt, The Three Musketeers, The Three Little Pigs, The Three Billy Goats Gruff, Goldilocks and the Three Bears, Three Blind Mice, and that most perfect and glorious configuration of all "an Englishman, an Irishman, and a Scotsman."

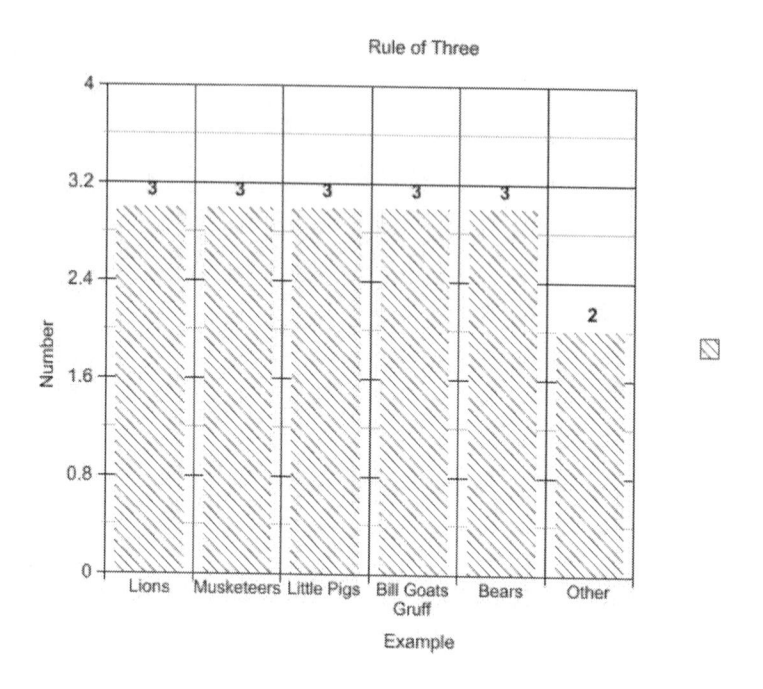

Rule of Three

Example	Number
Lions	3
Musketeers	3
Little Pigs	3
Bill Goats Gruff	3
Bears	3
Other	2

    Goldilocks and the Two Bears simply does not work. Its missing a sort of symmetry. It's missing a kind of harmony. It's missing... a bear.

    Things that come in threes are inherently more satisfying or more effective than other numbers of things. So there must be a Holy Ghost. The rule of three absolutely *demands* it.

Of course, one of the best examples of the power of the Rule of Three is in comedy. Three is the smallest number of points that can form a pattern, and comedians exploit the way our minds perceive expected patterns to throw you off track and make you laugh with the third thing they say.

Here's an old joke that illustrates that quite well:

"I can't think of anything worse after a night of drinking than waking up next to someone and not being able to remember their name, or how you met, or why they're dead."

Without the Rule of Three that gag simply wouldn't work. No wonder Arianism divided the Church completely. You can't have comedy without the Rule of Three, and you can't have religion without the Rule of Three.

Then there's Nominalism?

Nominalism says that everything in the world is purely conceptual. In other words existence exists, but only in the way that we construct it in our minds. So a tree is not a tree until we look at it, perceive it as something called a tree, and then use language to call it "a tree".

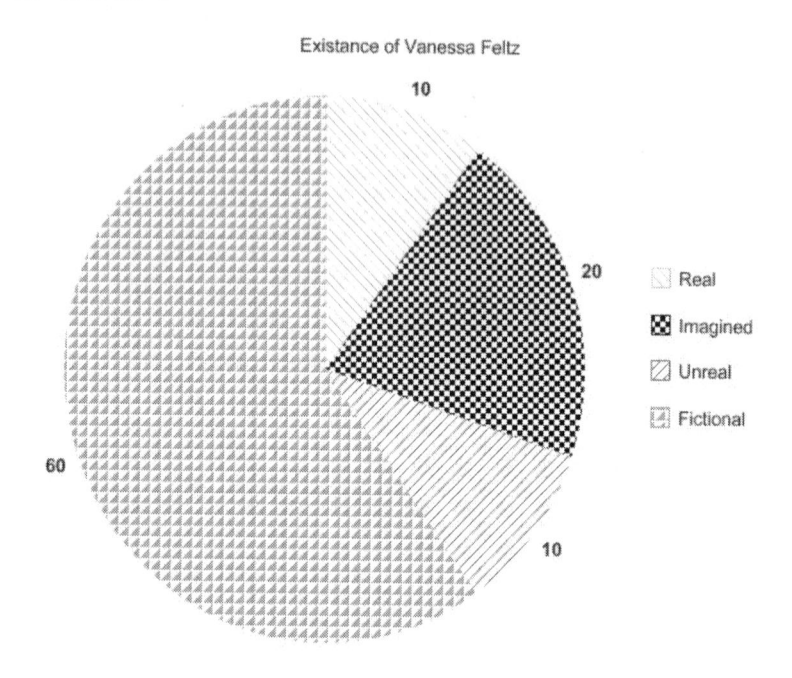

Existance of Vanessa Feltz

- Real: 10
- Imagined: 20
- Unreal: 10
- Fictional: 60

This means that Vanessa Feltz is purely conceptual. So if I don't look at Vanessa Feltz, and I don't perceive her to be Vanessa Feltz, and I don't give her the name Vanessa Feltz , then Vanessa Feltz does not exist. For this reason alone, I'm quite liking Nominalism.

Then there's The Church of the Flying Spaghetti Monster. This might sound like a joke but it's widely considered to be a real religion with its own philosophy and thousands and thousands of followers. Of course it has its opponents – most of them are fundamentalist Christians.

Followers of The Church of the Flying Spaghetti Monster call themselves Pastafarians. The only dogma allowed is the total rejection of dogma. So there are no strict rules and regulations.

There are also no ceremonies, no rituals and no prayers. Pastafarians are fond of beer, every Friday is a Religious Holiday, and they don't take themselves too seriously. Which all makes for a belief system that it's very easy to find alluring.

Basically, if you believe in Three Blind Mice and the Father, the Son and the Holy Ghost, you might as well believe in a Flying Spaghetti Monster.

OK, it breaks the Rule of Three, but there are an infinite number of ways for a Flying Spaghetti

Monster to exist, and only one way for it to not exist. So maths is firmly on its side.

Anyway, I know what you're thinking: Why didn't you just go and get the pogs out of dustbin? Well I did try, but garbage collection had already emptied the bins. Trust them to come on the right day. They had never done that before, and they have never, ever done it since. So my beloved pogs were gone forever.

Sue Whitstable taught me that you can do whatever you like, so long as it doesn't hurt anyone else and as long as it doesn't involve pogs. That's called Utilitarianism. I learnt about that during the last ten minutes of a Championship Play-Off semi final at Wembley Stadium.

It's the one simple premise that most Western society is based around. And the best bit is, you're allowed to hurt yourself as much as you want.

You're allowed to eat deep fried Mars Bars and drink gallons of Stella Artois and smoke sixty cigarettes a day and take part in extreme sports.

And if your doctor says you shouldn't do it, you can just say that's your choice! You're only hurting yourself, so it's fine.

That's called the Harm Principle. It increases happiness while at the same destroying well-being.

I decided to split with Sue Whitstable. She was destroying my well-being. I didn't need to take part in extreme sports. The extreme sport was living with Sue.

She was even giving me bad dreams. And I also began to experience a disturbing occurrence known as *déjà vue*. This is when you feel like you've seen or heard something before, but you can't quite put your finger on where or how or when it happened.

The Rule of Three.

Whatever the reason for it, *déjà vue* is a very, very disconcerting experience.

Of course, I realise that during the course of this piece, Sue Whitstable has been presented as a less than 3 dimensional character.

We've learned very little about Sue, other than she studied philosophy, made yoghurt and threw away my pogs. I would give you a fourth fact but that would break the Rule of Three, and then we'd be completely fucked.

There is actually a very good reason for Sue Whitstable coming across as being 2 dimensional. It's because I, along with most of the male authors on the planet Earth, are completely shit at writing female characters.

Suffice to say, and regardless of how two dimensionally I may have drawn this woman, Sue Whitstable made me unhappy. So unhappy that I was slowly eating and drinking myself to death. My own personal little Harm Principle.

Of course, it's entirely possible, indeed highly likely, that I might have done all of those things had she not been there at all.

5) Cat Not Here

My flat was now completely uncluttered. No philosophy books or floppy discs, or yoghurt pots under the bed. Ironically the place was now even emptier than it had been before - many of my own belongings having been ruthlessly thinned out during the bleak, Russian winter that was the Sue Whitstable regime.

The worry was that according to my newfound rules of the cosmos, that meant that my life was now more unstable than ever. I was further away from nice safe clutter and a step closer to nothingness.

The main benefit of our break-up was the toast. The toast was now fantastic. I was able to adjust the toaster to exactly the right setting and there was no-one there to creep into the kitchen and change it. No more burnt offerings. No more forced re-insertions due to disappointing under-toasting. There's nothing quite as good as break-up toast.

But unfortunately, toast is not enough. I was still unhappy. I was getting heavier and more unhealthy by the day. But then, a miracle happened.

Low fat Cheesy Wotsits were launched. There were also new low fat versions of many of my other favourite brands such as Quavers and Monster Munch.

Yes, praise be to Heaven, Walker's were now using Sunseed Oil. Which was a bit healthier. So now I could enjoy Cheesy Wotsits without feeling guilty. Only 95 calories in a bag. That's less than a hundred calories. That's less than a slice of bread.

And there was so much more to enjoy. Wotsits Quazers, Cheesy Squares and Walker's Salt & Vinegar French Fries. All with just 95 calories a bag. That's less than a slice of bread!

My local newsagent had to put up two extra shelves to cater for all the new types of crisp. Like everything else in the universe, cheesy snacks were defaulting towards multiple forms. Soon there would be millions of different types of cheesy snack.

Possibly billions. All of which would make the universe a safer and more stable place to live.

Cheesy Wotsits even had a Facebook page now. So I had a great place to meet new friends.

Nietzsche said "God is dead". He'd obviously never eaten low fat Cheesy Wotsits. When he said it, he was probably having a bad day, anyway. And, hey, why was the death of God so damned important anyway? 95 calories in a bag! That's less than a slice of bread!

Sue Whitstable would have reached for the remote control at this point, turned down Match of the Day, and explained it to me like this.

The Death of God was seen as the end of absolute morality. The very thing that the poor old Greeks had been working towards all those years ago. All those long hot nights with Socrates asking Plato complicated moral questions to which he probably already knew the answers. Now the world was somehow ready to kick all of that into touch.

Was God dead? Well to answer that question you first have to decide whether you believe God was ever alive in the first place. If you think he was at

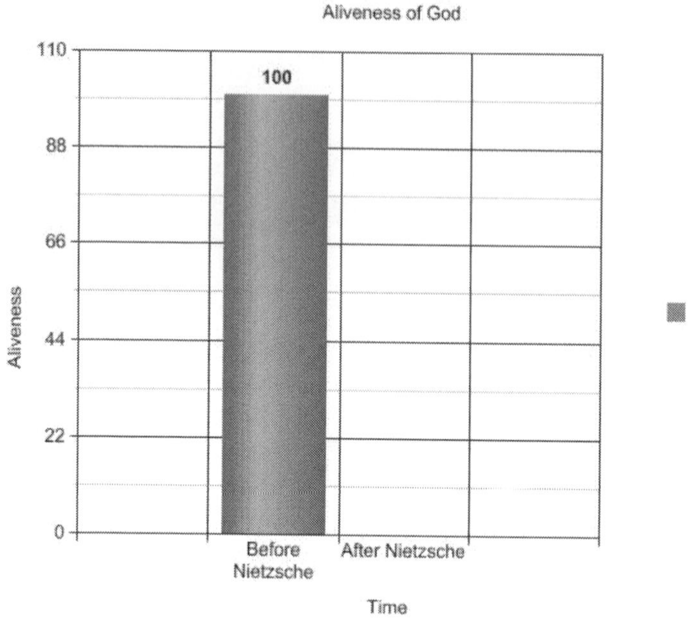

Aliveness of God
110
100
88
66
44
22
0
Aliveness
Before Nietzsche
After Nietzsche
Time

some point alive, then you are free to take a view on whether he's dead or not.

If you don't think God has ever existed then you cannot, with your hand on your heart, claim that he is now dead. How can he be?

Lets do the math. There are many ways in which God could be alive, but only one way that he could be dead. Worst case scenario is that he never existed *and* he's dead.

Karl Marx had already paved the way for Nietzsche by saying that moral values are only relative to the society in which we live. Now Nietzsche was saying that "God is dead" meant exactly the same thing – There was no absolute right or wrong. There was only people's *opinion* of right and wrong. And that was an infinitely moveable feast. It could change at any time. Like the rules in the Big Brother house. Or the settings on a toaster.

Sue Whitstable believed that there was no right or wrong at all, which technically made her what I now know is called a Relativist. That's why she thought it was OK to slap me in the face and thought it was fine to throw away my pogs.

I once asked Sue about that "kitten in a microwave" experiment. I said would it be OK to put her kitten in a microwave and she just said "Ooh, are you going to buy me a microwave?"
I think she was probably being Post-modernist. Sue often said that she was being Post-modernist, but

she never fully explained to me what that meant. As far as I understood it, post-modernism seemed to be an excuse for almost anything.

Me: "That comedian isn't funny."
Sue: "He doesn't have to be. That's post-modernist comedy."

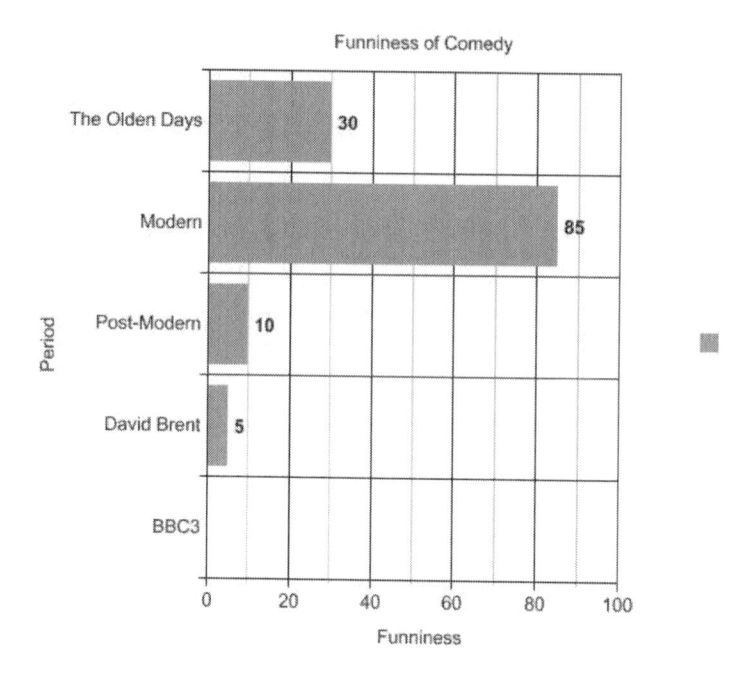

Funniness of Comedy

Period	Funniness
The Olden Days	30
Modern	85
Post-Modern	10
David Brent	5
BBC3	

Even philosophers don't seem to be able to agree on post-modernism. But then if they agreed with each other there wouldn't be anything for them to do anymore.

So if there is something called post-modernism, what was Modernism? For some reason Sue usually talked about Modernism when Manchester City were playing. Modernism said that science could save the world. Modernism got very excited about things like steel and concrete, and new gadgets like movie cameras and trains and cars.

Unfortunately Modernism also loved tanks and guns and rockets. Anything that went bang, basically. Two world wars later people weren't quite so enthusiastic about science, or about living in their shitty little modernist homes made out of metal and concrete. And so post-modernism was born.

Post-modernism is mostly about self-awareness. In *The Office,* for example, when they keep looking at the camera - that's post-modernism. It's deconstruction of television. It's about questioning everything you see. Everything that happens. It's also about the power of image over reality.

So, when we watch smart bombs flying down the chimneys of factories in Bagdad, live on BBC1, is that post-modern? Is that David Brent-style self-awareness that we're all in a real war and we know it?

When Tracy Emin exhibited her Unmade Bed in the Tate Modern and called it art, that was about as post-modern as you could possibly get. It was still shit. But that was the point. It was meant to be shit. It was so bad it was good.

Many things are so bad they are good. Jedward are so bad they are good. Other things are so good they are bad. Like opera, for example. Or ballet. At what point does perfection just become fucking annoying? But then I am a Philistine.

I briefly became a conceptual artist myself, once. I made a work called *Cat Not Here*. I said that I had created this piece of art in secret, then immediately destroyed it afterwards.

I then set up a web site and announced to the world that it was the very *absence* of the piece that I considered to be art.

I maintained that *Cat Not Here* could therefore be exhibited in art galleries and public spaces merely by being absent from them – but I insisted that the piece could only be absent from one place at a time.

Cat Not Here

Via its own web site the work was officially made available to be absent from selected art galleries, media centres, and public spaces throughout the year. There was a great response, and loads of feedback. Unfortunately, not much of it came from the art world. Only one real art gallery bought into the idea: The Gallery on the Square in St Ives.

The gallery's director Joni Farrington emailed me to say that she thought it was a "brilliant idea". The piece was subsequently officially absent from her gallery throughout March 2011.

I had some really inventive contributions to the web site. A visitor called Nick Kovari said, "I have been thinking about how a person might be able steal this piece of artwork. *Cat Not Here's* essence is in its non-existence, and therefore it cannot simply be taken away.

"So surely, the best way to steal it would be to to locate the spot that *Cat Not Here* currently occupies, and to place an actual cat in that spot. Would this not be art theft of the highest degree?"

Andy from Saudi Arabia wrote, "Is it only me that has seen through this shabby piece of shameless falsehood? This is merely an attempt to gain money and/or publicity by making bold and outrageous claims regarding the authenticity of an artwork?

"Should anyone care to examine it more closely, you can quite clearly see that it is not a cat, it is a llama that is not there. I fail to understand how so many so-called 'experts' did not spot this immediately!"

A very serious avant-garde gallery in Berlin sent me this very formal response to my request to not exhibit.

"Thank you for your exhibition proposal for the conceptual artwork *Cat Not Here* at Galerie Deadfly, Berlin. We are really interested in your project, however we are sorry to let you know that it isn't possible to have the project *Cat Not Here* absent from our gallery in the foreseeable future.

"The gallery has a forthcoming exhibition in September/October 2011 and due to the nature of this exhibition, we feel having your piece *Cat Not Here* absent from Galerie Deadfly prior to, or after this exhibition, would create a conceptual clash/ discrepancy, not only with our planned exhibition but with your proposed project too.

"Galerie Deadfly does not normally consider proposals to exhibit work or proposals not to exhibit work, but had the timing been different we would have really liked to have had your work *Cat Not Here* absent from our gallery. We thoroughly enjoyed looking at your website and especially liked the sound of *Fish Not Here* (2009).

"Although we are sorry not to be able to assist you with not exhibiting your work on this occasion, we hope you stay in touch regarding any information about *Cat Not Here* and any future projects. Yours Sincerely Galerie Deadfly.

My favourite feedback on the work was this email from Minneapolis:

"I would be very interested in not displaying your conceptual artwork *Cat Not Here* in my gallery. The piece is perfect for the venue and we are very excited by the opportunity to partner with you. We are *Gallery Not Here* in Minnesota.

"We are a conceptual gallery and do not exist. We are able to not display your work throughout March 2011, but would not be able to not display it after that as we have lots of other works of art which we will not be displaying. Space is extremely limited, as there is none.

"I am uniquely qualified to display this work in my gallery as I have no art training whatever.

However, my name is Art so that probably qualifies me by some kind of divine providence.

"Please let me know as soon as possible if you would like to partner with *Gallery Not Here* as we will have to arrange for transportation and storage."

Sincerely,
Art Brakob, PhD. Esq. C.I.A. MI-5, LOL.
Owner and proprietor of Gallery Not Here
Minneapolis, MN, U.S.A.

I unfortunately had to turn down this very generous offer as *Cat Not Here* was already booked throughout March 2011 to appear at that gallery in St. Ives.

A visitor called Geoff wrote simply, "Why don't you do a tour of *Brian Luff Not Here*. It would be funnier than if you were there and you'd probably get better attendance." Thanks for that, Geoff.

I was a little disappointed that more real galleries did not offer to display an absence of my work. I genuinely don't think that *Cat Not Here* has any less validity than, say, a lightbulb switching on and off in a room - a piece that won the Turner Prize for a man called Martin Creed.

Cat Not Here extracted all the remaining clutter from conceptual art and finally removed the need for it to exist at all. Unfortunately, in doing this it made the universe much more unstable and nudged it one step closer to nothingness.

The problem with Post-modernism is that it doesn't actually lead anywhere. It slams the door in our faces by saying that there're no absolute values by which we can judge or measure anything.

So, does that mean that all creative art is equally valid? Is *Cat Not Here* therefore on a par with the Mona Lisa or Van Gogh's *Sunflowers*? Surely not. But it would explain why art in general has become so completely fucking incomprehensible.

So screw Post-modernism. Perhaps all we need today is to get back to good old fashioned morality. But where are we going to find morality if God is dead? The internet?

On day you'll probably be able to buy morality in six packs from Tescos. God knows, you can get virtually everything else from there.

I never saw Sue Whitstable again. She met another mature philosophy student and they got married. I hear they now spend hours together playing Pogs. But they don't play for keeps.

When Sue asked to be my friend on Facebook I closed my account, leaving five hundred sheep to slowly starve to death in Farmville.

Since the introduction of low fat cheesy snacks, you'll be delighted to hear that I have lost something in the region of 4 pounds. I've never felt fitter and I'm thinking of applying to enter Slimmer of the Year.

Since I discovered that clutter is good I have trawled my way through hundreds of charity shops, car boot sales and bric-a-brac shops with the sole purpose of cluttering up my life with as much shit as I can get my hands on.

My flat is now filled with books I will never read, gadgets I will never use and chairs I will never sit on. I have mirrors I don't look in, lamps I don't switch on and CDs I will never play. I have a fish tank with no fish in it.

I have cigarette cards, bubblegum cards and beer mats. I have a collection of salt and pepper pots shaped like Siamese Cats. I have a collection of dead butterflies to rival the collection in the Natural History Museum.

I have a huge stuffed bear standing in the corner of the living room. Called Sue. But most of all I have thousands and thousands of pogs.

There are pogs on shelves, pogs in boxes and pogs in drawers. I have pogs in the freezer, next to the frozen Cheesy Wotsits.

So, why don't we all sit down together, have some toast, and have one last game of Pogs. But his will be no ordinary game of Pogs.

A chair I will never sit on.

On each of the pogs there will be a picture of a philosopher. Socrates, Plato, Aristotle...

We'll stack them all up and throw the slammer and see which philosophers land face up. To the beliefs and theories of those philosophers, and those philosophers alone, we will then entrust the future of life on this planet. Because philosophy really is that random. Or at least, it might as well be.

OK, now it's time for that big finish I've been promising you. For that we need to briefly return to our old friend Plato. Sue taught me that Plato was particularly interested in the immortality of the soul.

We argued a lot about this. Sue thought there was life after death. For me, that was always a complete contradiction. Surely there's either life *or* there's death.

My view used to be that the only life that exists after our deaths is the lives of the children we leave behind - the continuity of life that we pass on to the next generation through our genes. And if that was the case, what possible purpose would be served by our own selfish immortality?

But then I thought again. OK, we pass on our life force to our children. Job done. The species continues. So no need for the giver of that life to hang around indefinitely. You've done your bit, now fuck off.

But, what if our spirits, despite that knowledge, still insist on staying intact after our deaths, and they do stubbornly go and relocate to somewhere else?

Wouldn't that make those spirits little more than pointless clutter? Do you see where I'm going with this?

Throughout all of this, we have proposed that pointless clutter is the very thing that keeps the universe stable - the thing that protects the cosmos from nothingness?

What if there are an infinite number of ways for the soul to be immortal, but only one way for it to be dead. That would surely mean that mathematics is firmly on our side when it comes to proving the existence of the immortal soul. Wow! Maths proves there's life after death. That's what I *call* a big finish.

Philosophy is around us all the time in modern, everyday life. I saw a commercial recently for Sure deodorant. It invited viewers to attach a set of jingle bells to themselves so that they could see how much they move every day. This is almost worthy of Descartes: "I jingle, therefore I am."

It's also complete bollocks.

We're not encouraged to think enough. We are encouraged to soak up every piece of bullshit, homespun philosphy that is thrown at us. Go ahead, attach a set of jingle bells to yourself to see how much you move every day.

Or you could unzip your mind and think.

We don't actually need to be here at all. But mathematics assures us that it's physically impossible for the universe to not exist. So we're stuck with it.

Because in mathematics, as in philosophy, you can't not get *something*. Even if it's nothing.

Lewis Carroll said "Begin at the beginning, go on until you come to the end, then stop." So I'm going to stop now.

Anyone fancy a piece of toast?